DADS OR DUDS

(THE DIFFERENCE IS U)

Principles for Godly Fatherhood.

Ray Lagan

Written in conjunction with IRON SHARPENS IRON Men's Ministry

DADS OR DUDS
(THE DIFFERENCE IS U)

Dads or Duds (The Difference is U)

Copyright © 2011 by Raymond P Lagan

All rights reserved. No portion of this book may be reproduced, stored in a retrieval system, or transmitted in any form or by any means – electronic, mechanical, photocopy, recording, or any other – except for brief quotation in printed reviews, without the prior permission of the author.

All Scripture references included are from the
New International Version of the Bible.
ISBN – 978-1463535148

DADS OR DUDS

(THE DIFFERENCE IS U)

Volcanoes – What do you see?

Look at the front cover

Do you see a big useless waste of space that sticks out like a sore thumb and occasionally causes airline traffic problems?

Or do you see potential? Do you see energy? Do you see impact? Do you look past the surface of rock and search into the core? Deep inside at the heart of the volcano is the lava of change. If the volcanic inner juices are ever allowed to break out, our whole world experiences change.

Temperatures change, climates shift, land masses move, cities are radicalized; entire people groups can be impacted. Society and culture can reflect the power spewed forth for generations to come.

How do you see yourself as a Dad?

Are we as useless as a dormant volcano? Can we look inside ourselves, to go to our core and feel the heat and passion of who we really are deep down? Are we willing to be part of the plan to be released into our family's world?

If God created Dads as volcanoes of change for His glory, then He's calling on us to do our part in getting that eruption started. Review this study guide. Consider the readings, ponder and discuss the questions, practice some of the exercises. Be the stimulus God has outfitted you to be as a Dad so that your role can be fulfilled and your impact can be felt.

DADS OR DUDS

(THE DIFFERENCE IS U)

Dedication

To my parents and in-laws:

Joseph and Sophie Lagan,

Frederick and Gertrude Thielking.

They set the bar high. They taught with their patience

and years of unconditional love.

This Guide is my struggle to find words that describe their actions.

May the legacy continue!

Dads or Duds
(The Difference Is U)

Principles for Godly Fatherhood

Preface: The importance of Fathering is not where you start but where you end up. The odds are usually stacked against successful fatherhood. That doesn't have to be the end of the story. In this study we've created a repeatable format for success which you can apply in your group or alone.

There are 8 chapters with a unique principle in each one. Each chapter has 4 components and one extra WORK UP area for each principle. The format will be easy to follow and interact with. Let it be a guide and not a mandate. Use what's of value to stimulate the process of becoming a better Dad. You are impacting eternity!

The components are as follows.

 **WAKE UP** — General principle and copy of the applicable scripture.

 **WARM UP** — Interesting story, analogy, or data to stimulate thinking.

 **WISE UP** — Strategic questions that probe deeper for personal assessment.

 **WRAP UP** — Applications for the chapter review.

 **WORK UP** — Finish the work. Go to the next level.

DADS OR DUDS
(THE DIFFERENCE IS U)

Table of Contents

Chapter 1:	Spend Time	1-8
Chapter 2:	Keep Promises	9-16
Chapter 3:	Lead Well	17-24
Chapter 4:	Honor God	25-32
Chapter 5:	Stand Up	33-42
Chapter 6:	Be a Warrior	43-50
Chapter 7:	Honor Your Wife	51-58
Chapter 8:	Second Chances	59-66

Dads or Duds
(The Difference Is U)

Bringing children into the world is the easy part. Bringing them up Godly is the hard part. We all start out with a long stretch of time to become a great Dad. In this study we'll look at the characteristics of successful Dads. All Dads are called to follow a similar track.

The 8 weeks of study bring us face to face with these following realities as a Dad. The option of being a faithful DAD or a misguided DUD rests on each of us. The major difference is U (you).

1. Increased time = increased influence.
2. A promise kept lingers for a lifetime.
3. You will lead them.
4. Worship won't just happen.
5. Real Dads take a stand.
6. Worrier to Worshipper to Warrior.
7. Honor your wife for life.
8. Is it too late? – Too many mistakes.

(The Difference Is U)

Chapter 1

Spend Time

WAKE UP:

a. To influence others you need to spend time with them.

b. Mark 2:15 – 17

> While Jesus was having dinner at Levi's house, many tax collectors and "sinners" were eating with Him and His disciples, for there were many who followed Him. When the teachers of the law who were Pharisees saw Him eating with the "sinners" and tax collectors, they asked His disciples: "Why does He eat with tax collectors and 'sinners'?"
> On hearing this, Jesus said to them, "It is not the healthy who need a doctor, but the sick. I have not come to call the righteous, but sinners."

Jesus made an intentional effort to spend time with the sinners because that's whom He wanted to influence. His strategy was clear. You can't expect to speak into other's lives if they don't know you and see your life up close. He was willing to make that investment.

WARM UP:

You can't pick your parents, your date of birth, your economic condition when you were born or anything else regarding your history for that matter. You can't control how much or how little time your Dad spent with you. That's all history. What you have is what God ordained as a starting point. You can be thankful for it or angry about it or dismiss it or deny it, but it doesn't change anything. This is the starting point that God has scripted for you and it's from there that you will begin your fathering legacy.

Spend Time
(The Difference Is U)

It is from that starting point that we recognize where we are and what we have to do to make changes. Little changes can make a big difference.

The 212° Principle:

(One degree of change can make a huge difference)

Great men and women have often been inspired by a simple truth or single life changing event. That event triggers something in their life.

Sometimes the event is almost imperceptible, not noticeable until the changes start to take place. People call it the "Principle of 212°". You know it as the point that water boils. You see it as steam. You recognize it as a train going "full steam ahead", accomplishing the unthinkable simply because the water temperature increased one degree. At 211° degrees water would sit there all day and the train would never move. But find a way to increase to 212° and things start to happen. Men who read this study and work at applying it will see things start to happen. This guide can give you an eye for simple things that can take the core ingredients and give you the nudge to go to 212°.

Maybe you're the cause for things staying at 210° or 211°. Maybe you can be part of going to 212°.

SPEND TIME

(THE DIFFERENCE IS U)

WISE UP:

1. On a scale of 1 to 10 how badly do we really want to spend time with our kids?

   1   2   3   4   5   6   7   8   9   10

   Not at all   All the time

2. List the top 3 reasons we don't spend time with our kids.

3. What can I do to increase time with my children?

4. Is there a friend you would like to engage in this area and review each week to see how those time commitments are going? Who are some possibilities?

5. Did your Dad spend much time with you? When he did spend time, how valuable was it and why?

SPEND TIME
(THE DIFFERENCE IS U)

A Little Story

The businessman was at the pier of a small coastal Mexican village when a small boat with just one fisherman docked. Inside the small boat were several large Yellowfin tuna. The businessman complimented the Mexican on the quality of his fish and asked how long it took to catch them. The Mexican replied only a little while.

The businessman then asked why he didn't stay out longer and catch more fish? The Mexican said he had enough to support his family's immediate needs. The businessman then asked, "but what do you do with the rest of your time?" The Mexican fisherman said, "I sleep late, fish a little, play with my children, take a siesta with my wife, Maria, stroll into the village each evening where I sip wine and play guitar with my amigos; I have a full and busy life, señor."

The businessman scoffed, "I have a Harvard MBA and I could help you. You should spend more time fishing and with the proceeds buy a bigger boat. With the proceeds from the bigger boat you could buy several boats; eventually you would have a fleet of fishing boats. Instead of selling your catch to a middleman, you would sell directly to the processor and eventually open your own cannery. You would control the product, processing and distribution. You would need to leave this small coastal fishing village and move to Mexico City, then LA and eventually New York City where you would run your expanding enterprise."

The Mexican fisherman asked, "But señor, how long will this all take?" To which the businessman replied, "15-20 years." "But what then, señor?" The businessman laughed and said, "That's the best part! When the time is right you would announce an IPO and sell your company stock to the public and become very rich. You would make millions." "Millions, señor? Then what?" The businessman said, "Then you would retire. Move to a small coastal fishing village where you would sleep late, fish a little, play with your kids, take a siesta with your wife, stroll to the village in the evenings where you could sip wine and play your guitar with your amigos."

The fisherman, still smiling, looked up and said, "Isn't that what I'm doing right now?"

-Author Unknown

SPEND TIME
(The Difference Is U)

What can we learn about success from this story?

Do we need to rethink our definition of success?

WRAP UP:

Can you identify one person in your group you can team up with over the next few weeks to review and discuss your thoughts regarding spending time with your children as you progress through the study?

God didn't waste any time or talent in the development of your children. Whatever they have is God-ordained and can therefore be used by Him. Our role as Dads is to bring it out. We have to consider what is unique about our children. Ask God for insights to know how to:

Discover it: identify their uniqueness.

Develop it: work with them to grow these talents.

Deploy it: create avenues for them to use these talents.

Spend Time
(The Difference Is U)

WORK UP:

For going deeper this week you will need to study your child. Consider a topic of particular interest to your child and read or review a book about it. Be ready to start a conversation and discuss some highlights. Be intentional about starting a dinner conversation about something that interests someone else. Think of quality questions in advance of the discussion. For instance, if your child is intrigued by computer games, do some research on one. Prepare your thoughts and some intelligent questions for them in order to stimulate opinions and dialog. Avoid Yes / No questions, but instead solicit opinions such as:

What do you see as values for this game?

What emotions do you feel when you play this game?

How successful do you think this game will be and why?

SPEND TIME
(THE DIFFERENCE IS U)

Notes

SPEND TIME
(THE DIFFERENCE IS U)

Notes

KEEP PROMISES

(THE DIFFERENCE IS U)

Chapter 2

Keep Promises

WAKE UP:

a. A promise kept lingers for a lifetime. A promise broken lingers for a lifetime.

b. John 14:15-19 Jesus promises the Holy Spirit for each person who places faith and experiences new life. His promise is to never leave you.

> "If you love Me, you will obey what I command.. And I will ask the Father, and He will give you another Counselor to be with you forever— the Spirit of truth. The world cannot accept Him, because it neither sees Him nor knows Him. But you know Him, for He lives with you and will be in you. I will not leave you as orphans; I will come to you. Before long, the world will not see Me anymore, but you will see Me. Because I live, you also will live"
>
> ***Matthew 28:20*** = I am with you always

"And surely I am with you always, to the very end of the age."

WARM UP:

When Scott O'Grady was flying missions for the US Army over Bosnia in 1995, there was always the risk of being shot down over enemy territory. He went into flight knowing that risk. He had training which prepared him for that possibility. He ultimately faced that reality when his plane was hit and he was forced to eject over hostile territory.

KEEP PROMISES
(THE DIFFERENCE IS U)

O'Grady had received military training, a preflight briefing, and even special equipment for his flight in the event the unthinkable were to happen. On March 5, 2000, it did happen and all his training, briefing and equipment were called upon for survival. Even the best pre crisis preparation was over shadowed by the deep inside knowledge that his team was coming back for him. He served with the promise that they would never leave him. (He knew the motto "Go in together, fight together, come out together"). They flew as a team and he knew they would not leave one of their own behind. His external survival depended greatly on the precise use of his equipment and training. His emotional survival depended equally or more so, on the emotional knowledge that he was not alone. He was not forgotten and help was coming. He could keep on knowing the whole power of the United States military machine would be engaged in his rescue if he could hold his composure. He would live or die by that promise of his rescue.

Read the following excerpt from Time Magazine describing the rescue effort for O'Grady.

As the search continued through the night, the information was passed back to Washington where, six hours behind Central European Time, Clinton was receiving an evening briefing from National Security Adviser Anthony Lake. Clinton told Lake to keep him informed, but by the next morning the searchers still had not locked on to the lost pilot. "You know that matter we discussed last night?" said Lake at 9:30 a.m. "There's nothing more on that, and it looks uncertain." The President sighed and shook his head in frustration.

It would not be until early Thursday morning that Captain Thomas Hanford, an F-16 pilot from O'Grady's fighter wing making one of the repeated search sorties, received the first direct radio signal from the downed pilot. "Basher-52 reads you," said O'Grady, using the "call sign" that signifies a particular plane and its pilot. "I'm

alive; help." Hanford subsequently asked him to identify the name of the squadron in which he had served in Korea -- a question designed to ensure that O'Grady's message was not, in fact, a Serb trick. When he replied correctly, Hanford notified his superiors that he had made contact with O'Grady. Then he peeled away over the Adriatic to refuel. And for a few short moments, he let his emotions get the better of him. "It's hard to fly an airplane," he said later, "when you have tears rolling down your face."

The information was relayed to an intelligence-gathering AWACS circling high above, and then to Admiral Smith in London. He contacted Colonel Martin Berndt, commander of the 24th Marine Expeditionary Unit on the Kearsarge, a helicopter carrier sailing in the Adriatic. "What do you think?" asked the admiral. "I think we can get him," replied Berndt. Smith immediately gave the go-ahead, and Berndt roused 51 Marines-including 10 helicopter crewmembers-sleeping below decks; it was shortly after 3 a.m. At about the same time, Lake approached the President back in Washington, where it was around 9:30 p.m. "It looks real tonight," he said. "It looks like it's a go."

The rescue team would have preferred going in under cover of darkness, but by the time Smith's order came through, streaks of morning light were already appearing above the Dalmatian coast. At sunrise Berndt and his Marines, their faces covered with camouflage paint, had boarded a pair of enormous CH-53E Super Stallion helicopters-16-ton, seven-blade monsters. "We were so focused on the mission, I don't think anybody had any time to be nervous," recalls Berndt. "We were all excited that our young captain was alive and well."

Escorting the Stallions were two Marine AH-1W SuperCobra helicopter gunships, bristling with missiles, cannon and machine guns, and a pair of single-pilot Marine AV-8B Harrier jump jets. These six aircraft were backed up by identical sets of replacement helicopters and jump jets-none was needed-as well as two Navy EA-6B Prowler electronic warfare planes, two Marine F/A-18D

KEEP PROMISES
(THE DIFFERENCE IS U)

Hornets to provide air cover, and a pair of tank-killing Air Force A-10 Warthogs. The entire aerial armada of roughly 40 planes was choreographed from above by a nato awacs radar plane. "We had the whole shooting match up there," said Smith.

Scott O'Grady back in Serbia knew they were coming back for him. He had the promise of the US ARMY.

Go in together, Fight together, Come out together. That was the promise. The mission was a success; O'Grady made it back safely.

WISE UP:

1. Think of promises you have made and kept regarding your children.

   List a few here.

2. Were your children surprised when you did? Why?

3. Does the role of being a Promise Keeper and Godly father seem impossible / an unreachable goal?

KEEP PROMISES

(THE DIFFERENCE IS U)

4. Are you comfortable by the promise in John 14:15 regarding the Holy Spirit being available to us? How does this passage impact you?

5. Do you honestly consider God to be a Promise Keeper or just a Promise Maker? How strong is the connection between seeing God as a Promise Keeper and us being a Promise Keeper too?

6. True / False: My kids have confidence that if I make a promise or a commitment I will keep it and follow through.

7. On a scale of 1-10, how reliable would you like your kids to be when they give their word?
    1 2 3 4 5 6 7 8 9 10

8. True or False: If they don't keep their word, have we as parents become lulled into believing "that's just how kids are today, or that's the best I can do to impact my kids"?

Keep Promises
(The Difference Is U)

9. Rank the following reasons we use to describe our limitations in keeping our commitments with our kids from most prevalent to least.

   Lack of time

   Lack of money

   Lack of know how

   Lack of interest

   Lack of importance

   Lack of energy

Sometimes when we make a commitment it is helpful to involve a friend in that commitment. That simple act can give us very positive results.

   a. Since the friend is involved we may be more excited about keeping the commitment and God can use that to help us stay on track.

   b. Since we've invited someone outside the family there will be increased peer pressure to hit the mark.

   c. The friend can help as a gentle reminder before the event so that we don't forget details.

   d. Sometimes the friend has had some experience in that area that could help us get started.

   e. If he is holding you accountable he can see your level of commitment to keeping your word.

KEEP PROMISES
(THE DIFFERENCE IS U)

WRAP UP:

Here's a word of caution about making commitments; start small!

If you have a weak starting point for gaining your kids confidence be sure to start with little promises first and build up credibility over time. The lasting effect will be much greater and reliable if it's built over time and in small increments.

WORK UP:

For going to the next level this week, read Judges Chapter 7 and consider the feeling of Gideon as he led the Nation of Israel against an overwhelming army.

In the Old Testament we read of Gideon who had to trust God when he released his army down to 300 men against the 135,000 Midianites
(see Judges 7:5-8).

Being a Judge (like Gideon) at this time in the history of the nation of Israel was much like trying to be a successful Dad today. The demands are high and the odds are stacked against you. But we have God's promises to help us. Can He be trusted? If your kids see you trusting God to keep His word, they begin to trust you more as well. Don't let them down.

Take a challenge and go back through Judges Chapter 7 and make a list of key points and decisions Gideon had to make as he "built" his army. Do any of these types of decisions apply to you? (Consider issues like God's ability, and the size of your faith).

Pick one decision that may apply to you this week and ask God and a friend to help move you to a place of greater faith in that decision area.

KEEP PROMISES
(THE DIFFERENCE IS U)

Notes

LEAD WELL

(THE DIFFERENCE IS U)

Chapter 3
Lead Well

WAKE UP:

    a. You will lead them.

    b. Joshua 1: 1 - 6

> After the death of Moses the servant of the LORD, the LORD said to Joshua son of Nun, Moses' aide: "Moses My servant is dead. Now then, you and all these people, get ready to cross the Jordan River into the land I am about to give to them—to the Israelites. I will give you every place where you set your foot, as I promised Moses. Your territory will extend from the desert to Lebanon, and from the great river, the Euphrates—all the Hittite country—to the Mediterranean Sea in the west. No one will be able to stand against you all the days of your life. As I was with Moses, so I will be with you; I will never leave you nor forsake you. Be strong and courageous, because you will lead these people to inherit the land I swore to their ancestors to give them".

WARM UP:

In August 1914 one of the most extraordinary sagas of human adventure began in Great Britain as Ernest Shackleton and his team of 28 men launched the Transantarctic expedition with his ship called Endurance.

The explorers wanted to be the first to cross the unexplored continent of the Antarctic.

But when crisis struck 45 days into their expedition all the rules

Lead Well
(The Difference Is U)

changed. Now it was survival for him and his men. Leadership was now not just commanding a journey, it was fighting the odds or survival and maintaining the unity of the crew. Shackleton's leadership skills required him to work hard each day to stay one step ahead of his team and the events of the day. He awoke first. He took copious notes, he thought through all the "what if's" he may have to face before they became issues. His exploits have become a case study in crisis management in business schools today.

His men never doubted who was in charge or that Shackleton had a plan or that he would do everything possible to save them and the mission. They believed he had already considered all the options on their behalf so they willingly obeyed and followed his leadership.

Can our families say the same about us?

Authentic leadership is contagious. You don't have to recruit for it. If you're in a fire and one person can lead and finds a way out, you don't need to run an election to have people follow. They will desperately be running after him and his leadership.

Every family is literally trying to find the one to lead them out. Who is the one who knows the way? Prayerfully consider these 2 passages about your God given place in the home.

Ephesians 6:4. "Fathers do not exasperate your children; instead bring them up in training and instruction of the Lord."

Colossians 3:20 – 21. "Children obey your parents in everything, for this pleases the Lord. Fathers do not embitter your children, or they will become discouraged."

God has ordained you as the Dad to be that one for your family. The steering wheel is in your hand and the pedal is at your foot. Someone else can help read the map, but you are responsible to drive.

Make a plan and don't leave any doubt you are taking them somewhere good. Communicate that to them. If you do, they will follow you. They are God designed to want to do that.

LEAD WELL

(THE DIFFERENCE IS U)

WISE UP:

Reread Joshua Chapter 1. Consider Joshua's feelings at this time. Did he feel alone? Did he think God had a plan for Israel?

1. Does your family think you have a purpose and a plan for them?

    Do you? Can you explain it?

2. On a scale of 1 to 10, how easy is it for you to see areas in your family that need leadership attention?

3. Describe the value of writing out some objectives that you want to accomplish for the family this year. Make plans to share it with them. (Not a list of more things for them to do, but objectives that you will own. Remember the U in Dud).

4. True / false: I believe God has given me enough leadership skills to take charge of my family.

5. Describe the most powerful memory you have of taking the lead with the family. (Think of a family trip, a home improvement project, a sports event, a vacation etc).

6. How did your family respond to your leadership at that time?

Lead Well
(The Difference Is U)

7. Fill in the blank. The person I most admire for ability to lead others and take charge is _____.

8. What is it about that person that makes him so noteworthy as a leader?

9. Are his skills repeatable? Can specific lessons be learned from him?

10. Describe a time when you did not want to be the leader. What circumstances make it unpleasant? How does fear of those circumstances prevent you from taking the lead at home?

11. Can you name any rewards for a job well-done of leading the family?

12. With the plethora of leadership books and seminars available today, how do you think we are doing as a nation to train up strong leaders? Compare our generation to one generation ago in this category.

13. Why do you think leadership is so often abused? List 3 specific things men can do to ensure that leadership in the home stays balanced and healthy.

a.

b.

c.

WRAP UP:

No one is "born" with all the leadership skills he will ever need. Many people have strong leadership tendencies which can be developed. These types of people are always on the lookout for ways to improve. We need a similar mindset for taking care of our family. If we are to be faithful to the calling as fathers, we need to be vigilant in our pursuit of the tools of our trade. Let's not be too prideful or too lazy to learn a better way to lead. This is true even if we don't feel like leaders or aren't in leadership positions at our jobs.

Leadership doesn't mean knowing it all. It means being able to lead others in what you do know and taking responsibility to develop skills in the areas in which you need help.

LEAD WELL
(THE DIFFERENCE IS U)

WORK UP:

Consider spending time reading or watching a documentary about a leadership figure whom you greatly admire. You can read Joshua Chapter 3 and 4 if you need a starting point.

Based on your reading and study of this person, make a list of attributes this person exhibits which strengthens his/her ability to lead.

Consider what your life might look like if you were stronger in these areas.

Ask a friend candidly to give you feedback regarding your leadership skills and ask what areas may be lacking.

Create a personal list of areas to work on to improve leadership thinking. Ask your friend to weigh in regularly on your progress.

LEAD WELL
(THE DIFFERENCE IS U)

Notes

LEAD WELL
(THE DIFFERENCE IS U)

Notes

Chapter 4

Honor God

WAKE UP:

a. Connecting to God won't just happen.

b. Nehemiah 1: 3 - 9

> " They said to me, "Those who survived the exile and are back in the province are in great trouble and disgrace. The wall of Jerusalem is broken down, and its gates have been burned with fire."
> When I heard these things, I sat down and wept. For some days I mourned and fasted and prayed before the God of heaven. Then I said: "LORD, the God of heaven, the great and awesome God, who keeps his covenant of love with those who love Him and keep His commandments, let your ear be attentive and your eyes open to hear the prayer your servant is praying before you day and night for your servants, the people of Israel. I confess the sins we Israelites, including myself and my father's family, have committed against you. We have acted very wickedly toward you. We have not obeyed the commands, decrees and laws you gave your servant Moses.
> "Remember the instruction you gave your servant Moses, saying, 'If you are unfaithful, I will scatter you among the nations, but if you return to me and obey my commands, then even if your exiled people are at the farthest horizon, I will gather them from there and bring them to the place I have chosen as a dwelling for my Name.'

Honor God
(The Difference Is U)

WARM UP:

Nehemiah understood that assuming a leadership position for the nation of Israel meant starting on his knees. Then, he sat down and wept! He MOURNED and FASTED and PRAYED. It looked as if he was reading out of a different CEO manual than many of today's executive leaders do. They don't teach Nehemiah's approach at Harvard Business School for CEO leadership skills. That's not part of most executive training guides or business plans.

Many of us "middle agers" have lived through the bankruptcies of the likes, of Enron and WorldCom, and the financial meltdowns of some of New York's biggest financial institutions. Many of us suffered financial loss at the hands of corrupt management. We had senior management lining up to be first at the troughs for perks and financial rewards. We are devoid of many role models today showing us "Nehemiah like" leadership of humility and worship. So because the role models we have in public are giving us a distorted view of leading our businesses, we may have lost sight of how to lead our families.

Nehemiah knew that first to lead meant to be first to worship. He knew who he was before God and before man. He knew that to accomplish a God sized vision he wanted to be sure he had a God sized foundation. That meant leading his nation in putting God in proper perspective.

What would the distractors have said about Nehemiah and his dependence on God? I can hear their comments now:

- Don't give up your high position in the kingdom in case this project doesn't work out. (Remember Nehemiah was a high ranking government official as cup bearer to the King).

- Maybe you should start with something a little smaller or closer to home for your first project.

Honor God
(The Difference Is U)

- Don't you think the Israelites are losers? If they don't care enough about their own wall and gates why should you?

- There's a reason the city is so messed up. Don't get involved in what you don't know.

- Make sure you're getting your cut up front, because it may not be there later.

I'm sure Nehemiah asked himself a few questions as well. But the point is not what questions he asked, but what actions he took. God knows our frame and he knows we need to work through our doubts, questions, fears, and other emotions. But like Nehemiah, when we're all done with the questions we still need to act.

How do we define worship in our complex world today? Is it time spent at church or a small group we belong to? Is it singing at the beginning at church, but the sermon is not worship? Is it part of our personal devotion time? Can it be incorporated into our family time? Do we ever worship while on vacation? You can and should wrestle with these questions because your answers will dictate how your family sees your leadership. It seems to me there is a direct correlation between your ability to lead them in worship and your ability to lead them in life. I'm defining leadership here as setting guidelines, creating action items and being a role model. Let me say that another way.

If you are willing, able and equipped to lead your wife and children in worship (however you define it), it will be to that measure that you are able to lead in life. You will be the one leading them out of life's fire. It will be contagious and they will flock to follow you. God has designed them and you that way. I have never heard a wife say – "I want to leave my husband because he shows me and the kids too much of Christ love around the house and he won't stop leading us in worship."

Honor God
(The Difference Is U)

WISE UP:

1. What would "Nehemiah-like" leadership look like in your family today?

2. Has your wife or kids ever seen you weep or despair? Over what issue?

3. True/False: My kids would say I'm more concerned about a financial loss or business deal than an emotional concern for a loved one.

4. On a scale of 1 to 10, how well defined is my plan for my family in the area of connecting with God?

Honor God
(The Difference Is U)

5. Multiple choice:

    ___ My kids see me as leading the effort to connect with God around the house.

    ___ My kids have seen me personally connect with God around the house.

    ___ My kids rarely see me around the house.

6. What percent of my day is spent in intimate time with God? Normal answer is somewhere less than 1%. We have just not made it part of our Christian culture to have daily focus on worship. It's awkward and maybe embarrassing to set time aside for an activity we might define as worship. I wonder if we could be more effective by creating that as a priority in our day.

7. How do you think the rest of the world rates the US in terms of its spiritual commitment? Do you think we are viewed as more or less radical about our faith than many who are in opposition to our country today?
I certainly do not advocate their methods or goals, but they don't seem as concerned about their worship style seeming awkward or embarrassing.

Honor God
(The Difference Is U)

WRAP UP:

Start small – but start. Determine how God would be directing you to make committed time with God more a part of your daily routine.

Pray the Lord would at least give you a conviction regarding personal worship time and space.

Where will you meet with Him?

When will you meet with Him?

Ask your family if they will join you in some weekly venture that works for your family time and schedule which will increase the committed time with God in your home.

WORK UP:

Because you are not alone in the need to lead your family, engage the men from your small group or church with the challenge to worship. Be ready to share ideas of what works for you and your family. Be willing to listen and borrow ideas that work for others.

Be bold. Schedule a time for several families to get together and discuss what worship could be like for them as a group. Make it part of your next BBQ or softball game.

Solicit prayer support from other Dads who want to lead their families in this area. Ask them to support you as you consider some new radical way of worship for your family.

Spend some time in Deuteronomy chapter 6 and 7. How does this encourage you to include time with God in your daily life? Where and when does Moses suggest you talk about God with your family?

Honor God
(The Difference Is U)

Notes

HONOR GOD
(THE DIFFERENCE IS U)

Notes

STAND UP!

(The Difference Is U)

Chapter 5

Stand Up!

WAKE UP:

a. Real Dads Take a Stand.

b. Psalm 106: 28 – 31, Numbers 25: 1 - 13

> They yoked themselves to the Baal of Peor and ate sacrifices offered to lifeless gods; they aroused the LORD's anger by their wicked deeds, and a plague broke out among them. But Phinehas stood up and intervened, and the plague was checked. This was credited to him as righteousness for endless generations to come.
>
> These are the details in which Phineas stood up and intervened.
>
> While Israel was staying in Shittim, the men began to indulge in sexual immorality with Moabite women, who invited them to the sacrifices to their gods. The people ate the sacrificial meal and bowed down before these gods. So Israel yoked themselves to the Baal of Peor. And the LORD's anger burned against them.
>
> The LORD said to Moses, "Take all the leaders of these people, kill them and expose them in broad daylight before the LORD, so that the LORD's fierce anger may turn away from Israel."
>
> So Moses said to Israel's judges, "Each of you must put to death those of your people who have yoked themselves to the Baal of Peor."
>
> Then an Israelite man brought into the camp a Midianite woman

STAND UP!
(THE DIFFERENCE IS U)

> right before the eyes of Moses and the whole assembly of Israel while they were weeping at the entrance to the tent of meeting When Phinehas son of Eleazar, the son of Aaron, the priest, saw this, he left the assembly, took a spear in his hand and followed the Israelite into the tent. He drove the spear into both of them, right through the Israelite man and into the woman's stomach. Then the plague against the Israelites was stopped; but those who died in the plague numbered 24,000.
> The LORD said to Moses, "Phinehas son of Eleazar, the son of Aaron, the priest, has turned My anger away from the Israelites. Since he was as zealous for My honor among them as I am, I did not put an end to them in My zeal. Therefore tell him I am making My covenant of peace with him. He and his descendants will have a covenant of a lasting priesthood, because he was zealous for the honor of his God and made atonement for the Israelites."

WARM UP:

Most of us will never get called into service the way that Phinehas did. (glad about that). The point is that God is very serious about taking a stand when someone or something is getting in the way of our worship. We have to evaluate what we have let get into our families and the lives of our kids. Could God be calling us to take a stand on some family issues which we have let slide? Often times we say "it's not worth the battle that would ensue". We use that as a reason to not take any action. Based on what's happening at home, there are times when "it is worth the battle". It's worth the pain and exposure our family might face. It meant Phinehas would be seen in God's eyes as the one man who broke the plague. "This was credited to him as righteousness for generations to come." How would you like that on your tombstone? What stand would you want your kids to remember you for?

STAND UP!
(The Difference Is U)

Do you ever get tired of people telling you what you can do or not do? Sometimes we get lazy and don't even try something unless You Tube has an instructional video for it, or if it doesn't have the Underwriters Laboratory Seal of Approval. Authentic fatherhood will sometimes take us outside the "sure bets" and the "must do's". Sometimes we need to go against common wisdom of the day.

For example, in 1803 a man was born who was willing to go against the grain. He grew up in the Northeast and later moved to Texas to ranch cattle. He got involved in politics and was actually Mayor of San Antonia in the middle 1800's. He became a member of the State legislature and became very vocal. He also prospered as a rancher and owned over 300,000 acres of land. His real claim to fame however was his cattle. He refused to brand his cattle and any "unbranded cattle" he claimed were his. Whether he was an animal lover or just lazy is to be determined, but he would not brand his cattle. He was breaking social customs and the accepted method for doing business. He was willing to go against the norm. His name was Samuel A. Maverick. His name lives on today as someone who is willing to go against popular opinion and stand his ground. He was the original "maverick".

The old adage: "If you don't stand for something, you'll fall for anything" holds true in parenting as well as in anything else. The question is always: "Where do I draw the line? Where do I take a stand?"

Let me suggest one key issue we need to fight for. This may sound simplistic but where we draw the line is clear: "What does God want my family to be like?"

STAND UP!
(THE DIFFERENCE IS U)

He has put me in the car with this family. The steering wheel is in my hand and I control the gas and the brake. I get help reading the map and maybe a little with parking; but as for where we go and what happens to us when we get there, that's my role, me, (Dad). The buck stops here! So I have to ask the question, "What does God want my children to look like?"

What does this look like in my family?

WISE UP:

1. Try to recall the last time you had to confront the kids (or your wife) on a spiritual issue in your house. List some words to best describe the scenario:

Warm, engaging, healthy, constructive,

Or:

Painful, embarrassing, divisive,

Maybe:

Inflammatory, abusive, spiritual...other?

2. On a scale of 1 to 10: How well did you handle the situation? Were you clear about what you were standing up for, and why?

   1 2 3 4 5 6 7 8 9 10

Stand Up!
(The Difference Is U)

3. Could you use Scripture to support the stand you took?

4. What would you do differently this time if you had to readdress the issue?

5. True / False : Did you encounter increased spiritual anxiety as you prepared to take the stand?

Consider enlisting some "back up" prayer support from other men when you go into this type of battle. These are often spiritual battles and warfare will break out when we go on the offensive against enemy territory where we may have yielded in the past.

6. Did you experience any of the following reactions from your family as an initial response to your stand?

    A. It's not fair.

    B. No one else is doing it this way.

    C. I'm old enough to make my own decisions.

    D. That's "old school" thinking.

    E. You just don't understand.

STAND UP!

(THE DIFFERENCE IS U)

7. How did you handle the response from family as the issue was being addressed?

8. Yes / No: Would you do it again?

WRAP UP:

God will hopefully never ask you to take a stand that will require you to take a human life (like Phinehas); but He already has called you into service to take a stand to make a difference in the lives of your children.

Some words of caution here:

I don't believe we need to go on the warpath looking for "stands to take". This should be God-ordained. He will direct your paths to know what to confront and when. Let me also encourage you to have scripture to support the position you are taking. Not legalism, but standing your ground is much easier if you believe it comes from the Word and not made up by man.

We learned as parents there are times we make mistakes and go overboard on some issues or parameters we are setting. We learned to give our children the right to respectfully ask us this question, when they felt unjustly addressed.

STAND UP!
(The Difference Is U)

The question is: " Is this open for discussion?" Around our house, we know that to be a trigger question which causes us to pause for consideration.

It's not an automatic "get out of jail free" card but when used with discernment by our kids they realized we would stop and listen to ourselves to determine if we were being unjust in our stand. The kids did not over use it so the medicine was still potent enough to stop us and get us thinking. Of course we seldom changed our position on the issue, but it was great for the kids to know we were taking their perspective into account. They felt they were being heard and on the occasion where we had overacted, we could apply the "open for discussion option to correct our position."

Hey, parents are people too.

WORK UP:

Taking a stand within the family is a great start for communicating to the ones we love that Godly living is important to us. We need to do that in the home. We also need to do that within our church, our community and within our government. This will look a little different for each of us, but let's break some new ground. There are regular occasions for Christian families to be more visible in the community. Perhaps as a family, consider writing a Christ-centered editorial response to some current event in your community. Occasionally, the State Capital or Town Hall will be the site for an organized rally to express our God-given concerns about education, government or social situations. Find out when the next one is scheduled and commit to attending. Set the role model for your family by inviting them to attend with you.

Maybe the school board is sponsoring an open house to discuss new curriculum or dress code policies, etc. Let your voice be heard. This needs to be done appropriately and politely, of course, but exercise the right to represent the Christian morals and ethics that you want for your family.

STAND UP!
(THE DIFFERENCE IS U)

Put the Joshua 24:15 passage to work: "choose for yourself whom you will serve, but as for me and my house, we will serve the Lord." Go public with your commitment and take a visible stand!

To assist you in gaining strength in this area memorize Joshua 24:14 – 15.

STAND UP!
(THE DIFFERENCE IS U)

Notes

Stand Up!
(The Difference Is U)
Notes

BE A WARRIOR

(THE DIFFERENCE IS U)

Chapter 6

Be a Warrior.

WAKE UP:

a. Worrier to Worshipper to Warrior.
b. Judges 6: 2 - 12.

> " Because the power of Midian was so oppressive, the Israelites prepared shelters for themselves in mountain clefts, caves and strongholds. Whenever the Israelites planted their crops, the Midianites, Amalekites and other eastern peoples invaded the country. They camped on the land and ruined the crops all the way to Gaza and did not spare a living thing for Israel, neither sheep nor cattle nor donkeys. They came up with their livestock and their tents like swarms of locusts. It was impossible to count the men and their camels; they invaded the land to ravage it. Midian so impoverished the Israelites that they cried out to the Lord for help.
>
> When the Israelites cried to the Lord because of Midian, he sent them a prophet, who said, "This is what the Lord, the God of Israel, says: I brought you up out of Egypt, out of the land of slavery. I snatched you from the power of Egypt and from the hand of all your oppressors. I drove them from before you and gave you their land. I said to you, 'I am the Lord your God; do not worship the gods of the Amorites, in whose land you live.' But you have not listened to Me."
>
> The angel of the Lord came and sat down under the oak in Ophrah that belonged to Joash the Abiezrite, where his son Gideon was threshing wheat in a winepress to keep it from the Midianites. When the angel of the Lord appeared to Gideon, he said, <u>"The Lord is with you, mighty warrior."</u>

Be a Warrior

(The Difference Is U)

WARM UP:

In the passage we just read, is God reaching out to Gideon as a first step? It's safe to say that Gideon is stuck. You can see details of that conversation with God's angel in the rest of Chapter 6 and Chapter 7 of Judges.

Gideon is like most Dads today, stuck in place and trying to go it alone. Too often we give up and become content with marginal fatherhood. That's not good enough. God wants more! So do you! That's why you're investing time in this study. God is not satisfied with Dads who check out of fatherhood when mom and the baby check out of the maternity ward. We're talking about being Dad as a long-haul commitment.

Being a Judge (like Gideon) at this time in the history of the nation of Israel, is much like trying to be a successful Dad today. The demands are high and the odds are stacked against you.

a. Rough circumstances to start with.

b. Bad habits to break.

c. Evil influences seem to have already won the hearts of our kids and our culture.

d. God's expectations remain unchanged.

The good news here is that God continues to commit to be with us in the struggle and He does send help. You can see more of that in the WORK UP section at the end of this chapter.

Be a Warrior

(The Difference Is U)

WISE UP:

1. Why does Gideon feel so helpless against the Midiantes? (vs 2- 6)

2. Would you describe yourself today as more of a "worrier" or a "warrior" for your family? What circumstances in your world cause you to feel helpless in the role of being a Godly father?

   What makes you want to cry out to God?

It was over 50 years ago (May 25, 1961) that President Kennedy challenged the US to win the race to the moon. It would be draining on all fronts. It would challenge all limits of the day in the field of science. It was completely uncharted territory and was considered impossible by many Americans of the day.

We look back now with the confidence of success in overcoming the odds. We are challenged in a similar way today to do the impossible. Take back the family and lives of our children from the destructive influences that surround them. The task is overwhelming. We often times don't know what to do first or next. But just as we did with the vast requirements of space exploration we need to take the first step. Then follow one step at a time as we move in on the goal.

3. How did Gideon respond to their "impossible" situation? (Judges Chap 6:6)

4. What if Israel had the same "can do" attitude regarding their circumstances?

5. How did God respond? (vs 7 – 10)

Which option best describes their response to God? (vs 10)

a. No obedience - Did not listen and did not obey.

b. Some obedience – Listened selectively and obeyed a little.

c. Complete obedience – Listened attentively and obeyed completely.

6. So they know why they are in the situation they are in. Do you think they have become lulled into believing: "Oh well, this is just how things are?"   (The Eeyore complex from Winnie the Pooh).

Yes or No. Explain Why.

BE A WARRIOR

(THE DIFFERENCE IS U)

7. On a scale of 1 to 10, how Godly is our land today?
   1   2   3   4   5   6   7   8   9   10

8. True or False: Have we, as parents, become lulled into believing "that's just how kids are today, or that's the best I can do to impact my kids"?

9. How important are your feelings in deciding when to go to battle?

10. Describe the feeling when someone labels you as really good at something? (vs 12)

11. Have you found yourself trying hard to live up to the expectations someone else has for you?

WRAP UP:

Most of you are familiar with the annual ritual known as "March Madness". It is the college basketball annual bracketing buzz and count to the Final Four. What's interesting is among all the basketball

Be a Warrior

(The Difference Is U)

rah rah for the week, the biggest college story this year is actually revolving around the sport of NCAA wrestling. In Philadelphia, where the finals were being held, a wrestler from Arizona State just won the national championship at the 125lbs weight division. His name is Anthony Robles, and he went against all the odds. Just like Gideon when no one thought he had a chance to defeat the Midianites because he was greatly outnumbered, no one expected Robles to win. His opponent Matt McDonough was last year's National Champ and looked poised to win again. But again, just like Gideon this event was the culmination of years of preparation. Here is where the wrestler would take a stand. Since Robles was very young everyone told him this victory was impossible. As a warrior at heart he refused to believe that and went forward in faith and confidence. His convictions held out as he won the match 7 - 0, as the crowd rose to their feet to cheer him on. What's so special about the new National champ? He was born without a right leg.

So Gideon faced impossible odds, and so did Anthony Robles, and in some ways, so do you. But nothing is impossible with God and the faith to lead our family to the next victory. Each victory is accomplished one at a time. What impossible challenges do you face this week, and what's your strategy for Godly success?

WORK UP:

Read the rest of Chapter 6 and 7 of Judges to get a full appreciation for the transition that Gideon (and the family of Israel) went through. Notice the patience of God to move him through the stages of development. After being very honest with yourself regarding your current bravery quotient, commit to move forward. Commit to stand up and make war if needed against the forces that attack your family. Fight for the food and safety of your children and freedom to worship freely. Think hard about the forces that attack your home on a daily basis and wipe you out. Now determine a plan for victory and enlist

BE A WARRIOR
(THE DIFFERENCE IS U)

strong men to fight with you in the battle for your family. You won't win this battle on your own strength. (God made sure that Gideon knew that when he winnowed the army down to 300.) But you won't win the battle at all unless you draw a line in the sand and refuse to let anyone or anything take your family from you. I challenge you to Stand Up!

    a. Make a list of current challenges facing you and each member of your family.

    b. Begin discussing a plan with each individual member to ensure victory.

BE A WARRIOR

(THE DIFFERENCE IS U)

Notes

HONOR YOUR WIFE

(THE DIFFERENCE IS U)

Chapter 7

Honor Your Wife.

WAKE UP:

a. Great Dads Honor Their Wives

b. Genesis 1: 1 – 31, 2:18.

The Beginning

> In the beginning God created the heavens and the earth. Now the earth was formless and empty, darkness was over the surface of the deep, and the Spirit of God was hovering over the waters. And God said, "Let there be light," and there was light. God saw that the light was good, and He separated the light from the darkness. God called the light "day," and the darkness He called "night." And there was evening, and there was morning—the first day.
>
> And God said, "Let there be a vault between the waters to separate water from water." So God made the vault and separated the water under the vault from the water above it. And it was so. God called the vault "sky." And there was evening, and there was morning—the second day.
>
> And God said, "Let the water under the sky be gathered to one place, and let dry ground appear." And it was so. God called the dry ground "land," and the gathered waters He called "seas." And God saw that it was good. Then God said, "Let the land produce vegetation: seed-bearing plants and trees on the land that bear fruit with seed in it, according to their various kinds." And it was so. The land produced vegetation: plants bearing seed according to their kinds and trees bearing fruit with

Honor Your Wife
(The Difference Is U)

seed in it according to their kinds. And God saw that it was good. And there was evening, and there was morning—the third day.

And God said, "Let there be lights in the vault of the sky to separate the day from the night, and let them serve as signs to mark sacred times, and days and years, and let there be lights in the vault of the sky to give light on the earth." And it was so. God made two great lights—the greater light to govern the day and the lesser light to govern the night. He also made the stars. God set them in the vault of the sky to give light on the earth, to govern the day and the night, and to separate light from darkness. And God saw that it was good. And there was evening, and there was morning—the fourth day.

And God said, "Let the water teem with living creatures, and let birds fly above the earth across the vault of the sky." So God created the great creatures of the sea and every living thing with which the water teems and that moves about in it, according to their kinds, and every winged bird according to its kind. And God saw that it was good. God blessed them and said, "Be fruitful and increase in number and fill the water in the seas, and let the birds increase on the earth." And there was evening, and there was morning—the fifth day.

And God said, "Let the land produce living creatures according to their kinds: the livestock, the creatures that move along the ground, and the wild animals, each according to its kind." And it was so. God made the wild animals according to their kinds, the livestock according to their kinds, and all the creatures that move along the ground according to their kinds. And God saw that it was good. Then God said, "Let us make mankind in Our image, in Our likeness, so that they may rule over the fish in the sea and the birds in the sky, over the livestock and all the wild animals, and over all the creatures that move along the ground."

Honor Your Wife
(The Difference Is U)

> So God created mankind in His own image, in the image of God he created them; male and female He created them.
>
> God blessed them and said to them, "Be fruitful and increase in number; fill the earth and subdue it. Rule over the fish in the sea and the birds in the sky and over every living creature that moves on the ground." Then God said, "I give you every seed-bearing plant on the face of the whole earth and every tree that has fruit with seed in it. They will be yours for food. And to all the beasts of the earth and all the birds in the sky and all the creatures that move along the ground—everything that has the breath of life in it—I give every green plant for food." And it was so. God saw all that He had made, and it was very good. And there was evening, and there was morning—the sixth day.
>
> Chapter 2: 18 The LORD God said, "It is not good for the man to be alone. I will make a helper suitable for him."

> **_WARNING:_** The pastor general has warned that reading this chapter may be hazardous to your comfort. It is not recommended for men who are very content in their current opinions and mindsets. It can cause change in attitudes and daily actions and could disrupt your current schedule at home. It is not recommended that you share this content with your wife unless you really care about improving your marriage!

Honor Your Wife
(The Difference Is U)

WARM UP:

I remember thinking what a terrific wife I had. It seemed God picked me to have a great marriage partner while so many others were not so blessed. Even with the great wife God had given me, I remember thinking if only I could work out these few other wrinkles in my wife she would really be perfect. If I could lovingly get her to think in a particular way and change the way she handled this situation or thought about some things we would have it made. It seemed if only she would change her approach to some issues (which I had great clarity on) she would be perfect.

I am quite humbled as I recall the experience I had of God revealing my supreme arrogance on this topic. I was preparing some thoughts to share with my church when God directed me to Genesis Chapter 1 and the creation story. He gently but unquestionably pointed out some key concepts to me regarding my thinking. It seemed perfectly clear to me that if my wife would change this attribute and that characteristic about her feelings and thinking she would be perfect. If only she could change some of her quirky ways to think more like a man, we would have it made. I'm talking about issues like style of communication, approach to problem solving, lack of emotion when making decisions, etc.

Like a train at full speed, God allowed me to get hit with His truth. Upon reading His word, I learned that He had designed her with those special quirks. He had ordained that she would approach things that way. She would think differently from the way I would <u>by design</u>. She was woman. I was man. And God saw it as VERY GOOD. How could so different be so very good? It would be much more efficient (I thought) if she would approach things in my pattern. But again God said His way was VERY GOOD. It wasn't just good, or just better than my idea. It was VERY GOOD.

In Genesis 2:18 in the retelling of the creating story God saw what He made in man and said – "it is NOT GOOD that man should be alone."

Honor Your Wife
(The Difference Is U)

In Genesis 1:4, 10, 12, 18, 21 and 25 – God emphasizes a major point about His creation. How does God describe the separation of the land and the water?

How does God describe the land producing vegetation?

Then in Genesis 1:31 – He created woman and it was VERY GOOD. Notice the added emphasis. Implication is man alone is not good, everything created by itself is good and woman created along with man is VERY GOOD. Therefore His perfect design includes woman, as she was designed, not as my interpretation of what would be most efficient or effective.

So God, you mean – the most efficient is not the always the best? (Nope – think Israel wandering for 40 years) or that making us have a long conversation on a simple issue is part of your design? (Yep – you're getting to know one another).

Or just listening and not trying to fix what's being discussed (as if we could anyway) is God's design. (Yes, yes, yes).

Slowly I'm getting it….

The bulk of this chapter is about honoring your wives and not addressing your role as Dad. However, this area is one of the primary pillars of being a Godly Dad. If we don't get this right, the stool only has 2 legs. The kids will see through you faster than a lit fuse on a firecracker. For the sake of being a Dad and not a dud, let's get this right.

Honor Your Wife

(The Difference Is U)

WISE UP:

True / False questions:

1. My initial reaction to most discussions with my wife is "I'm right, I already know the answer", if only she would see it my way this would all be cleared up.

2. The major source of conflict around our home is my wife's inability to see things my way.

3. I have found myself trying to fix a problem my wife shared with me when all I needed to do was listen to it.

4. On a scale of 1 to 10 how much does my wife feel honored by me in my ability to value her opinion and her approach to issues?

   1 2 3 4 5 6 7 8 9 10

5. When was the last time you and the guys poked fun at the way our wives dealt with an issue? What does that communicate about our opinion of God's "VERY GOOD" design?

6. Do you think the children have ever heard you dismiss your wife's opinion as second rate? What does that communicate to them about your respect for her?

Honor Your Wife
(The Difference Is U)

7. How would your male friends rate you in this area of appreciating your wife and her insights and approaches?

WRAP UP:

Take some time to reread the creation story in Genesis Chapter 1 and 2 and ask God to open your eyes to the marvel of His creation. Ask him to reveal His strategy for uniquely creating man and woman. Answer the question: why it is NOT GOOD that man should be alone.?

WORK UP:

Be intentional this week about reading the Genesis passages <u>with your wife.</u> Explain to her the conclusions you have drawn from this study. Describe the impact that should have on your marriage.

If she is still conscious after hearing your revelation, ask her to comment on this "Not good", "Good", "Very Good" scenario that God created.

Be bold and ask your wife to help you intentionally discuss some family concern with this new perspective.

Ask your wife, "what it would look like to her to be valued by you in your relationship".

Commit to making a list of ways you can show her honor and value. Consider asking some friends to check in with you in this area in the coming weeks.

Honor Your Wife
(The Difference Is U)

Notes

Chapter 8
God of the Second Chances

WAKE UP:

a. Is it too late? I made so many mistakes.
b. Joshua 2:18 - 21 , Joshua 6:23 – 25, Matthew 1:5 – 6.

> Now the men had said to her, "This oath you made us swear will not be binding on us unless, when we enter the land, you have tied this scarlet cord in the window through which you let us down, and unless you have brought your father and mother, your brothers and all your family into your house. If any of them go outside your house into the street, their blood will be on their own heads; we will not be responsible. As for those who are in the house with you, their blood will be on our head if a hand is laid on them. But if you tell what we are doing, we will be released from the oath you made us swear."
>
> "Agreed," she replied. "Let it be as you say."

So she sent them away, and they departed. And she tied the scarlet cord in the window.

Four Chapters later in Joshua 6...

> Joshua said to the two men who had spied out the land, "Go into the prostitute's house and bring her out and all who belong to her, in accordance with your oath to her." So the young men who had done the spying went in and brought out Rahab, her father and mother, her brothers and sisters and all who belonged to her. They brought out her entire family and put them in a place outside the camp of Israel.

GOD OF THE SECOND CHANCES
(THE DIFFERENCE IS U)

> Then they burned the whole city and everything in it, but they put the silver and gold and the articles of bronze and iron into the treasury of the LORD's house. But Joshua spared Rahab the prostitute, with her family and all who belonged to her, because she hid the men Joshua had sent as spies to Jericho—and she lives among the Israelites to this day.
>
> And the conclusion in Matthew 1:5 – 6.
> Salmon the father of Boaz, whose mother was Rahab,
>
> Boaz the father of Obed, whose mother was Ruth,
>
> Obed the father of Jesse,
>
> and Jesse the father of King David.

WARM UP:

Ever just want to be somebody else? Hit the reset button and start over? Just like the deadwood button at the bowling alley, you hit the switch and all the broken promises, shattered dreams, missed opportunities, bad choices and downed pins of life are moved away and your life becomes clean again. But what if you really messed up? What if your bad choices have now resulted in consequences for life? What if your secret is out and you can no longer pretend to be something that you are not anyway?

Now you are real, now you are raw, now you are ready, now you are Rahab!
Go back 3500 years and the only thing standing in the way of Israel becoming a nation was a fully trained army, a well-stocked city, and a 30-foot thick wall. God's frisky people were waiting outside in overflow parking outside Jericho and hoping that Joshua had a plan. He did! It was clever! Basically he was going to be obedient to whatever God told him to do. Pretty good strategy, huh?

God of the Second Chances
(The Difference Is U)

Back to Rehab. God can use the most basic ingredients when He wants to make changes. Just like Joshua leading the Israelites, Rahab needed to choose obedience. We read in Joshua 2:18 – 21 the spies cut a deal with Rahab – her silence for her safety. She hangs a red rope from her window until Israel storms the place. Rahab and her family receive a "get out of Jericho free" card. They do pass GO and collect their freedom and a new beginning. Rahab continues in her path of obedience and we see some startling results.

Look ahead in Matthew 1:4 – 6. Here we see she marries a man named Salmon. They have a son named Boaz who marries a lady named Ruth who has a grandson named Jesse and he has a son we call King David. What was her secret sauce that allowed for her cataclysmic conversion in a catastrophic event? One word – obedience! Did she have past regrets? Did she have present day doubts? Did she have weak knees when the walls started shaking and falling down around her and her family? I'm quite sure the answer is, yes. But here is the key: she had practiced obedience (hanging a red rope from her window) and a very simple faith (waited for the spies to come rescue her from chaos). Even though the fireworks had started and her home was literally crumpling around her, she waited patiently for the spies and her rescue. (See Josh 6:22 – 25 for details).

So where are you today? Have you made a few bad choices? A few decisions you regret? Do you have a label you would like to change? Is your world getting a little shaky (job, finances, family, healthcare)?

Let's start by making a few decisions for simple obedience and give the Lord opportunity to show up and rescue us. Most of us won't have to search too long to discover what Step 1 of obedience would look like in our lives.

I'm sure Rahab had no regrets when the dust literally settled. She looked back at what she was then and compared it to who she is now. Her old world vs her new world. She had lost her home, her

God of the Second Chances
(The Difference Is U)

savings, her friends, her old associates and her old reputation. Her nation was wiped out. She gained a "do-over", a new start to life, an experience of obedience which now brought her "a future and a hope." (Jeremiah 29:11). Not a bad trade for saying "yes" to God.

WISE UP:

1. Can you identify at least one major habit or trend in your life which you wish you had never started?

2. If there were a master "reset" switch you could pull to change some life choices you have made, could you identify what you would change?

3. True or False: I believe it's too late in my life for even God to correct my circumstances.

GOD OF THE SECOND CHANCES
(THE DIFFERENCE IS U)

4. What's the scariest part about practicing major steps of obedience?

    a. It brings my current sins out in the open.

    b. It may impact other people in my family.

    c. What if God doesn't "come through" and help me complete the changes?

    d. I don't believe it will make any lasting difference.

    e. God doesn't care anyway.

    f. God could keep asking me to make other changes once I get started.

5. On a scale of 1 to 10, how much better could my life be if I began to make changes?

6. True or False – I don't believe God is a God of second chances?

WRAP UP:

We can never give up and stop pursuing God. He is a God of the second chances and He evidenced this throughout recorded history of the Bible.

Just review these brief passages for continued insight into His promises. Don't take these verses out of context. They are not saying, and I am not implying that life will be a stroll in the park. But I am

God of the Second Chances
(The Difference Is U)

saying as long as you are breathing God is not done with you yet. He will give you a chance and all the resources you need to be effective for what He wants done through you. That's called a second chance.

Josh 29: 17 – He gives us a future and a hope.

John 10:10 – I have come so you may have life in abundance.

WORK UP:

Don't believe the lies that society gives out. Our world tells us, "if you're not the biggest, brightest, and strongest or best, you don't have value." Experience is the process of making bad decisions through which we learn to make good decisions. All of us need to hit the "reset button" on some areas of life. We should not keep resetting however.

To go deeper this week, determine the key areas that you would want to take back and do over.

If necessary confess those to God and draw up a strategy to correct what might have gone wrong. Don't leave it there.

After you have made things right with God and corrected as much as possible in your path, move forward with the wisdom of experience. Do something to help others from making the same mistake.

Using your energy to be part of the solution is the most therapeutic work you can do. This is your first chance to make the second chance your best chance to please God.

GOD OF THE SECOND CHANCES
(THE DIFFERENCE IS U)

Notes

GOD OF THE SECOND CHANCES
(THE DIFFERENCE IS U)

Notes

Made in the USA
Charleston, SC
25 August 2011